JOEY MYERS

From Clutter to Cash: The Entrepreneur's Guide to Junk Removal

First published by KDP 2024

Copyright © 2024 by Joey Myers

All rights reserved. No part of this publication may be reproduced, stored or transmitted in any form or by any means, electronic, mechanical, photocopying, recording, scanning, or otherwise without written permission from the publisher. It is illegal to copy this book, post it to a website, or distribute it by any other means without permission.

First edition

ISBN: 9798323411085

Advisor: Shawn Wolf

This book was professionally typeset on Reedsy.
Find out more at reedsy.com

Contents

Chapter 1: Understanding the Junk Removal Industry   1
Chapter 2: Starting Your Junk Removal Business   12
Chapter 3: Operational Strategies   24
Chapter 4: Marketing and Customer Acquisition   34
Chapter 5: Niche Opportunities in Junk Removal   44
Chapter 6: Technology in Junk Removal   51
Chapter 7: Scaling Your Business   59
Chapter 8: Sustainability Practices   64
Chapter 9: Financial Management   69
Chapter 10: Future Trends and Preparing for Change   74
Conclusion: Harnessing the Right Tools and Partnerships for...   79

Chapter 1: Understanding the Junk Removal Industry

Introduction to Chapter 1

Welcome to the dynamic world of junk removal—a sector that might not glitter but is gold nonetheless for those who know how to navigate its waters. This chapter delves deep into what makes the junk removal industry tick, from its broad market dynamics to the intricate dance of regulation and innovation. As we peel back the layers, you'll gain insights not just into how the industry operates today, but how you can position yourself for success in the cluttered spaces of tomorrow.

1.1 Market Overview

In the ever-expanding universe of waste management, junk removal services shine as a beacon of growth and opportunity. The industry, often overshadowed by its larger waste management cousins, has carved out a niche that responds with agility to the needs of urban and suburban landscapes alike. It's a market driven by increasing consumer awareness around sustainability and the growing trends in home improvement and urban development.

Junk removal, once seen as a simple service, has transformed into an eco-conscious and customer-focused industry. Businesses and consumers are more aware than ever of the environmental impacts of waste, propelling junk removal companies that prioritize recycling and responsible disposal methods to the forefront. This shift is reflected in the steady increase in demand for junk removal services, as households and companies seek to declutter responsibly.

The market is also witnessing a surge in competition, from small, locally-owned outfits to major players like Waste Management, which dominate the landscape with comprehensive junk removal and recycling services. This competition drives innovation and service diversification, including specializations in electronic waste, appliance removal, and hazardous materials, catering to a broader spectrum of customer needs.

Furthermore, technology plays a pivotal role in reshaping the industry. Platforms like ClutterQuote revolutionize how services are rendered, offering streamlined, customer-friendly solutions that enhance booking efficiency and job management. With features that allow customers to snap a photo and receive an instant quote, the barriers between service request and execution are thinner than ever.

Key Takeaways:

- **Growth and Sustainability:** The junk removal market is growing, driven by environmental concerns and the increasing clutter of modern life.
- **Competitive Landscape:** Understanding your competitors and the services they offer can help you find your niche and capitalize on unaddressed needs.
- **Technological Integration:** Embracing technology, like instant booking platforms, can significantly enhance customer satisfaction and operational efficiency.

By understanding these market dynamics, junk removal entrepreneurs can better strategize their entry or expansion in the industry, ensuring they not only add value but also thrive in an increasingly competitive environment. In the next section, we will explore the key players who dominate this field and how a new entrant might carve out their own space.

1.2 Key Players and Competition

Navigating the junk removal industry requires a clear understanding of its key players and the competitive dynamics that shape the landscape. As we explore this sector, it becomes evident that both large-scale operators and nimble, local businesses play critical roles. Their strategies, strengths, and weaknesses define the opportunities and challenges for anyone looking to carve out a niche in this market.

Large-Scale Operators: Dominating the Field

At the top of the food chain are the behemoths like Waste Management and Republic Services, which not only offer junk removal but a full spectrum of waste management services. These companies benefit from widespread brand recognition, extensive networks, and significant resources for marketing and technology. They set industry standards and are often the first choice for both residential and commercial clients due to their reliability and comprehensive service offerings.

However, their size can also be a disadvantage. Larger companies often lack the flexibility to adapt quickly to local market changes or innovate in ways that disrupt their established service models. This opens doors for smaller competitors who can specialize in niche areas or offer more personalized services.

Mid-Sized Competitors: Agile and Customer-Focused

Mid-sized companies often fill the gap between large operators and small, local businesses. They typically have the resources to invest in technology and staff training but maintain a level of flexibility that larger companies cannot match. These businesses can quickly adapt to new trends, such as eco-friendly junk removal practices, and often focus on customer relationships to build loyalty.

For example, companies like Junk King and 1-800-GOT-JUNK? operate nationally but use local franchises to maintain a community-focused approach. They leverage brand recognition while adapting to the specific needs of local markets. These franchises often excel in customer service, which can be a significant differentiator in the industry.

Local Players: Community Roots and Specialized Services

Local junk removal businesses are the industry's backbone, deeply rooted in their communities and highly responsive to local needs. They often thrive by offering specialized services that larger companies do not, such as furniture restoration or specialized recycling options. These businesses build strong customer relationships through personal touch and community involvement, which can be compelling to residents and local businesses alike.

Moreover, local operators are typically more agile in changing their business models or adopting new technologies. They are quick to collaborate with tech platforms like ClutterQuote, which provides tools for smart scheduling and quick quote generation, enhancing their competitiveness against larger firms.

Navigating Competitive Pressures

In such a diverse marketplace, understanding competitive pressures is crucial. Price competition can be fierce, with companies often undercutting each other to gain market share. However, competing on price alone is a risky strategy that can compromise service quality and business sustainability.

Instead, successful companies focus on differentiating their services—be it through eco-friendly disposal methods, superior customer service, or innovative use of technology. They also pay close attention to operational efficiency, optimizing routes and job schedules to reduce costs and improve service speed.

Strategic Alliances and Technological Advancements

Strategic alliances, either through partnerships with recycling centers or technology platforms like ClutterQuote, can enhance a company's service offerings and operational efficiency. For example, partnerships with local charities for item donations not only help the environment and community but also build a positive brand image.

Technology, too, plays a pivotal role. Advanced scheduling software, customer relationship management (CRM) systems, and mobile apps can streamline operations and enhance customer interactions. These tools are invaluable for managing the complexities of scheduling, route optimization, and customer communication, which are crucial for efficiency and scalability.

Key Takeaways:

- **Understanding Competitors:** Knowing who the key players are and what they offer provides insights into how to position your business effectively.
- **Differentiation is Key:** In a competitive market, distinguishing your services can attract more clients and build lasting relationships.
- **Leverage Technology and Partnerships:** Utilizing advanced technologies and forming strategic alliances can significantly enhance operational efficiency and customer satisfaction.

As we move forward, we'll delve into the regulatory environment that shapes this industry. Knowing the rules of the game is essential for ensuring compliance and seizing opportunities that arise from legislative changes.

1.3 Regulatory Environment

Navigating the regulatory landscape is a critical aspect of managing a successful junk removal business. Compliance with local, state, and federal regulations not only ensures legal operations but can also offer competitive advantages by positioning the company as a responsible and trustworthy service provider. This section explores the various regulatory frameworks that influence the junk removal industry and offers strategies to effectively manage compliance.

Understanding the Regulatory Spectrum

The junk removal industry faces a complex array of regulations that can vary significantly from one jurisdiction to another. At the federal level, regulations primarily focus on environmental protection and safety, governed by agencies such as the Environmental Protection Agency (EPA) and the Occupational Safety and Health Administration (OSHA). These regulations ensure that waste is disposed of in a manner that minimizes environmental impact and that workers operate in safe conditions.

State and local regulations can be more prescriptive, covering aspects such as licensing, vehicle operation, and specific types of waste handling. For instance, certain states have stringent rules about the disposal of electronic waste (e-waste), requiring special handling and recycling processes. Additionally, local municipalities may have ordinances that dictate when and where junk removal operations can occur, including restrictions on noise levels and operational hours.

Key Regulations to Consider

1. **Hazardous Waste Management**: Many items that might appear in junk removal, such as batteries, paint, and electronics, are classified as

hazardous and require specific disposal procedures. Failure to properly manage hazardous waste can lead to significant fines and legal issues.
2. **Vehicle Regulations**: Junk removal businesses rely heavily on their fleet of vehicles, which must comply with state and federal transportation laws. This includes regulations on vehicle emissions, safety standards, and transport permits for hauling certain types of waste.
3. **Employment Laws**: As with any business, junk removal companies must adhere to employment laws, including those related to wages, hours, and working conditions. This is particularly important given the physically demanding nature of junk removal work, which can also pose safety risks.
4. **Local Zoning and Permitting**: Local zoning laws may affect where junk removal businesses can base their operations and where they can dispose of collected items. Permits may also be required for operating in certain areas or for disposing of waste in local landfills.

Strategies for Compliance

Maintaining compliance requires a proactive approach. Here are some strategies that can help junk removal businesses navigate the regulatory landscape effectively:

- **Stay Informed**: Regulations can change frequently, and staying informed is crucial. Subscribing to industry newsletters, joining relevant associations, and attending seminars can help businesses keep up with changes.
- **Build Relationships with Regulators**: Establishing a positive relationship with local regulators can be beneficial. Regular communication can help clarify requirements and demonstrate the company's commitment to compliance.
- **Invest in Training**: Employee training programs that focus on safety, hazardous waste handling, and other regulatory requirements are essential. Well-trained employees are less likely to make costly mistakes that could lead to regulatory violations.
- **Leverage Technology**: Technology can help manage compliance effec-

tively. For example, software that tracks the disposal of hazardous waste can ensure proper documentation and help businesses avoid violations.
- **Consult with Experts**: Sometimes, the best approach is to consult with legal or environmental experts who specialize in regulatory compliance. This can be particularly useful for complex issues or when entering new markets.

Key Takeaways:

- **Comprehensive Understanding of Regulations**: Knowing and understanding the full spectrum of applicable regulations is crucial for operational legality and efficiency.
- **Proactive Compliance Management**: Implementing proactive strategies for compliance can mitigate risks and enhance business reputation.
- **Continuous Education and Improvement**: Regular training and updates are essential to keep pace with changing regulations and to ensure that all levels of the organization understand their roles in compliance.

In the next section, we will explore the opportunities and challenges that currently face the junk removal industry, providing a deeper understanding of how businesses can navigate these factors to enhance growth and sustainability.

1.4 Opportunities and Challenges

The junk removal industry, like any other, is rife with both opportunities and challenges. Entrepreneurs who can effectively navigate these waters will find fertile ground for innovation and growth. This section discusses key opportunities that can drive business expansion and sustainability, as well as significant challenges that entrepreneurs must address to ensure long-term success.

CHAPTER 1: UNDERSTANDING THE JUNK REMOVAL INDUSTRY

Opportunities for Growth and Innovation

1. **Expanding Environmental Awareness**: The growing societal focus on sustainability is a major opportunity for junk removal businesses. As consumers and corporations alike seek to reduce their environmental footprint, services that emphasize recycling and responsible disposal of waste are increasingly favored. Companies that can effectively market their eco-friendly practices, such as high recycling rates or partnerships with environmental organizations, can differentiate themselves from competitors.
2. **Technological Integration**: Technology can streamline many aspects of the junk removal business, from logistics and scheduling to customer management and billing. Innovations such as GPS tracking for efficient routing, on-demand mobile applications for quick service booking, and CRM systems for better customer interaction and retention are just a few examples. Businesses that leverage these technologies can improve efficiency, reduce costs, and enhance customer satisfaction.
3. **Diversification of Services**: Junk removal companies that diversify their services to include related offerings such as moving services, shredding, or the sale of refurbished items can tap into additional revenue streams. This not only helps to cushion the business against slow periods but also meets the broader needs of their customer base.
4. **Corporate and Government Contracts**: While residential services are a staple for junk removal businesses, securing contracts with commercial and government entities can provide stable, long-term revenue. These organizations often have ongoing needs for waste management, and securing such contracts can lead to significant business growth.

Challenges to Overcome

1. **Regulatory Compliance**: As discussed in the previous section, navigating the complex web of regulations that govern waste management can be daunting. Compliance is not only about avoiding fines but also

about building credibility and trust with customers who are increasingly concerned about ethical disposal practices.
2. **High Operational Costs**: Junk removal is a logistics-heavy business, involving significant costs related to transportation, labor, and disposal fees. Fuel prices, vehicle maintenance, and the cost of disposing of waste at landfills or recycling centers can fluctuate, impacting profitability. Efficient route planning, investment in fuel-efficient or electric vehicles, and effective job scheduling are critical to managing these costs.
3. **Competition**: The barrier to entry in the junk removal industry can be relatively low, leading to intense competition. New entrants must find ways to differentiate themselves, whether through pricing, niche services, or superior customer service. Building a brand that stands out requires strategic marketing and a clear value proposition.
4. **Customer Acquisition and Retention**: Attracting and retaining customers is a fundamental challenge. The one-time nature of many junk removal jobs means that businesses must continually attract new customers while also encouraging repeat business. Effective online marketing, positive customer reviews, and referral programs can be key strategies for building a loyal customer base.
5. **Economic Sensitivity**: The demand for junk removal services can be sensitive to economic cycles. During economic downturns, both businesses and consumers may cut back on spending, which can include postponing or canceling non-essential services like junk removal. Diversifying the service offering and maintaining flexible pricing can help mitigate these risks.

Key Takeaways:

- **Capitalize on Eco-Friendly Trends**: Emphasizing sustainable practices can attract customers who are conscious of their environmental impact.
- **Embrace Technology**: Integrating advanced technologies can lead to significant improvements in operational efficiency and customer engagement.

- **Expand Service Offerings**: Diversification can protect against market volatility and open up new revenue channels.
- **Focus on Competitive Differentiation**: In a crowded market, clearly differentiated services or exceptional customer experiences can help your business stand out.

As we transition into the practical steps of starting a junk removal business, it's important to consider these opportunities and challenges in your strategic planning. This will ensure that your business is not only prepared to navigate the complexities of the industry but is also positioned for sustainable growth and success.

Chapter 2: Starting Your Junk Removal Business

Introduction to Chapter 2

As you venture into the junk removal industry, starting your own business is both an exciting and daunting task. This chapter is designed to guide you through the foundational steps of setting up a successful junk removal business. From crafting a robust business plan to understanding the necessary tools and licenses, each section is crafted to equip you with the essential knowledge and tools needed for your entrepreneurial journey.

2.1 Business Planning

The backbone of any successful business is a well-thought-out business plan. For a junk removal business, this plan not only serves as a roadmap for operation but also as a crucial tool for securing financing and guiding your business through its initial years.

The Components of a Strong Business Plan

1. **Executive Summary**: This opening section provides a concise overview

of your business and your plans. It should include your business name, the services you offer, and a brief description of your objectives.

2. **Business Description**: Offer more detailed information about your junk removal business, including the legal structure (e.g., sole proprietorship, LLC), the specific types of services you'll provide, and the characteristics that make your business unique.
3. **Market Analysis**: Analyze your local market to understand the demand for junk removal services. This should include an assessment of local competitors, target demographics, and potential market size. Highlight trends such as increasing environmental awareness or local construction booms that could influence demand.
4. **Organizational Structure**: Describe the management and personnel structure of your business. Who will manage the business? What roles will you need to hire for, and what will their responsibilities be?
5. **Sales and Marketing Strategy**: Outline how you will attract and retain customers. This might include strategies for digital marketing, partnerships with local businesses, promotional offers, or community engagement practices.
6. **Service Line**: Detail the types of junk removal services you plan to offer. Will you specialize in residential or commercial services? Will you offer related services such as recycling or selling reusable items?
7. **Funding Request**: If you are seeking financing, specify the amount needed and how it will be used. Detail whether you are seeking debt or equity financing and the terms you'd expect.
8. **Financial Projections**: Provide financial forecasts, including projected income statements, balance sheets, and cash flow statements for the next three to five years. These projections should be optimistic but realistic.
9. **Appendices**: Include any additional information that will help establish the credibility of your business plan, such as key resumes, product pictures, legal agreements, or market research data.

Strategies for Effective Business Planning

- **Understand Your Audience**: Whether your business plan is intended for internal guidance or for securing external funding, understanding your audience is crucial. Tailor your language, detail, and presented data accordingly.
- **Research Thoroughly**: Your market analysis should be backed by solid data. Understand local regulations, disposal fees, and the competitive landscape to ensure realistic and comprehensive planning.
- **Plan for Scalability**: Consider how your business can grow in the future. This might involve plans for geographic expansion, adding additional services, or scaling up your team and equipment.

Key Takeaways:

- **Blueprint for Success**: A well-crafted business plan is your first major step towards establishing a successful junk removal business.
- **Guide for Operations and Funding**: Use your business plan as a guide for day-to-day operations and as a necessary tool for securing funding.
- **Foundation for Future Growth**: Ensure your business plan allows room for growth and adaptability as your business evolves.

In the next section, we will delve into financing your venture, exploring various options for funding your startup and operational needs. Understanding your financing options is crucial for a smooth launch and sustainable growth.

2.2 Financing Your Venture

Securing adequate financing is a crucial step in launching your junk removal business. It ensures that you have the necessary funds to cover startup costs, purchase essential equipment, and maintain operations until the business becomes self-sustaining. This section explores various funding options available to you and provides guidance on choosing the most appropriate ones based on your business needs and circumstances.

Understanding Startup Costs

Before seeking financing, it's important to understand the costs involved in starting a junk removal business. These can include:

1. **Vehicles**: You'll need reliable vehicles, such as trucks or vans, capable of hauling junk. These could be new or used, depending on your budget.
2. **Equipment**: Essential tools might include gloves, shovels, rakes, bins, and potentially more specialized equipment depending on the services you offer (e.g., heavy lifting equipment for furniture removal).
3. **Licenses and Permits**: Costs for acquiring the necessary business licenses and permits vary by location but must be accounted for.
4. **Insurance**: Liability and vehicle insurance are critical to protect your business and employees.
5. **Marketing**: Initial marketing expenses may include website development, social media advertising, and traditional marketing materials like flyers and business cards.
6. **Rent and Utilities**: If you're not operating from home, you'll need a location for storing vehicles and other equipment.
7. **Salaries and Wages**: If you plan to hire employees, you need to account for wages from the start.

Financing Options

Once you have a clear understanding of the startup costs, you can explore various financing options:

1. **Personal Savings**: Many entrepreneurs start their businesses using personal funds. This option avoids debt but may risk your personal financial stability.
2. **Bank Loans**: Traditional bank loans are a common source of funding.

They typically offer lower interest rates and longer repayment terms. However, they require a solid business plan and good credit history.
3. **Small Business Administration (SBA) Loans**: In the United States, the SBA offers several loan programs designed to assist new and existing businesses. These loans are often easier to qualify for than traditional bank loans and come with favorable terms.
4. **Business Line of Credit**: This is a flexible option that allows you to borrow up to a certain limit and pay interest only on the portion of money that you use. It's useful for managing cash flow and unexpected expenses.
5. **Equipment Financing**: Specific loans for purchasing business equipment can often be secured by the equipment itself as collateral.
6. **Angel Investors and Venture Capitalists**: These are individuals or firms that invest in startup businesses in exchange for equity. They are suitable for businesses that plan to scale quickly.
7. **Crowdfunding**: Platforms like Kickstarter or Indiegogo allow you to raise small amounts of money from a large number of people, typically in exchange for providing them with a product or service later.
8. **Grants**: Some government agencies and private foundations offer grants to small businesses, particularly those in eco-friendly sectors.

Choosing the Right Financing Mix

Choosing the right type of financing involves weighing the pros and cons of each option against your business needs:

- **Risk Tolerance**: How much personal financial risk are you willing to take? Using personal savings or collateralizing personal assets can be risky.
- **Cost of Capital**: Loans need to be repaid with interest. Compare the cost of capital and ensure it doesn't eat too much into your profits.
- **Control of Your Business**: Equity investors may want a say in how you run your business. If you prefer full control, loans might be a better option.
- **Cash Flow Considerations**: Ensure that the repayment terms of any borrowed money align with your expected cash flow. This is crucial to

avoid cash crunches.

Key Takeaways:

- **Comprehensive Budget Planning**: Start with a clear understanding of your initial costs to determine how much funding you need.
- **Diverse Funding Sources**: Consider a mix of different funding sources to balance risk.
- **Strategic Financial Planning**: Choose financing options that align with your business goals and cash flow projections.

Armed with the right financial resources, you can ensure a strong start for your junk removal business. Next, we will look at the essential equipment and tools needed to operate your business efficiently.

2.3 Equipment and Tools

For a junk removal business, having the right equipment and tools is not just about efficiency; it's about safety, service quality, and the ability to handle a wide range of jobs effectively. This section will guide you through the essential equipment and tools needed to start and operate your junk removal business, ensuring you are well-prepared to meet the demands of the job.

Vehicles for Transport

The most significant investment in terms of equipment for a junk removal business will likely be your vehicles. These are essential for transporting junk from clients' properties to disposal facilities or recycling centers.

1. **Trucks**: A durable and reliable truck is the backbone of any junk removal business. Depending on your budget and needs, you might start with a

used truck to save on initial costs. Trucks with a large capacity and easy loading features, such as a box truck with a lift gate, are ideal.
2. **Trailers**: For expanding capacity or handling larger jobs, trailers can be a cost-effective solution. They can be attached to your primary truck, increasing your haulage without the need for an additional vehicle.

Loading Tools and Materials

Efficient loading and unloading of junk are crucial for operational efficiency. The right tools can also prevent injury, making these investments important from a safety perspective as well.

1. **Dollies and Hand Trucks**: These are essential for moving heavy items like furniture, appliances, and large boxes. Specialty dollies for stairs or uneven surfaces can also be valuable.
2. **Tarps and Straps**: To secure loads during transport and protect items from damage, sturdy tarps and straps are necessary. These tools help ensure that items don't shift during transit, reducing the risk of damage or accidents.
3. **Shovels, Rakes, and Brooms**: Basic tools for clearing debris, sweeping, and ensuring that you leave client sites clean and tidy. This attention to detail can greatly enhance customer satisfaction.

Personal Protective Equipment (PPE)

Safety must be a priority in the junk removal business. The right personal protective equipment helps prevent injuries and ensures that your team can work comfortably and safely.

1. **Gloves**: Heavy-duty gloves protect hands from sharp objects, hazardous materials, and general wear from handling rough materials.
2. **Boots**: Durable work boots with slip-resistant soles and ankle support are important, especially when lifting heavy items or working in potentially

hazardous environments.

3. **Eye Protection**: Safety goggles or glasses are necessary when dealing with potentially hazardous materials or during demolition-type removals.
4. **Ear Protection**: For jobs that involve loud noise, such as operating heavy machinery or power tools, ear protection is essential to prevent hearing damage.

Technological Tools

Incorporating technology can streamline operations, enhance customer service, and improve overall efficiency.

1. **Software Solutions**: Invest in reliable CRM software to manage customer relationships, scheduling software to efficiently plan jobs, and invoicing software to handle billing and payments smoothly.
2. **Mobile Devices**: Equipping your team with smartphones or tablets can help them stay connected, access scheduling information, navigate to job sites, and update job statuses in real-time.

Miscellaneous Supplies

A few additional supplies will ensure you're prepared for various customer needs and can handle unexpected situations.

1. **Cleaning Supplies**: Keeping basic cleaning supplies on hand, such as garbage bags, disinfectants, and air fresheners, allows you to provide additional cleaning services if required.
2. **Tool Kit**: A basic tool kit can be invaluable for quickly dismantling furniture or handling minor repairs at a job site.
3. **First Aid Kit**: Always have a first aid kit readily available in each vehicle to handle any minor injuries that might occur on the job.

Key Takeaways:

- **Invest in Quality**: While it can be tempting to cut costs on equipment, investing in high-quality, durable tools can save money in the long run through reduced maintenance and replacement costs.
- **Safety First**: Prioritize safety to protect your team and avoid potential liabilities.
- **Leverage Technology**: Use technology to enhance operational efficiency and customer satisfaction.

Equipped with the right tools and understanding how to utilize them effectively sets the foundation for a successful junk removal business. In the following section, we'll explore the necessary licensing and permits, ensuring your business operates legally and meets all regulatory requirements.

2.4 Licensing and Permits

Ensuring that your junk removal business is fully licensed and has all the necessary permits is not just a legal requirement—it's a fundamental aspect of establishing trust with your customers and protecting your business from legal issues. This section will guide you through the various types of licenses and permits you may need, along with insights on how to obtain them.

Understanding the Importance of Proper Licensing

Operating without the required licenses and permits can lead to serious consequences, including fines, business closure, and a damaged reputation. Compliance demonstrates professionalism and commitment to lawful business practices, which can significantly enhance your company's credibility and marketability.

CHAPTER 2: STARTING YOUR JUNK REMOVAL BUSINESS

Types of Licenses and Permits Required

The specific licenses and permits required can vary depending on the location of your business and the services you offer. Generally, these can include:

1. **Business License**: Almost all jurisdictions require businesses to have a general business license to operate legally. This license needs to be renewed periodically, usually annually.
2. **DOT Number**: If your junk removal business uses heavy-duty vehicles, you might need a Department of Transportation (DOT) number. This is especially true if you are crossing state lines. The DOT number serves as a unique identifier for your vehicles and is used to monitor your company's safety information during inspections, audits, and compliance reviews.
3. **Waste Carrier License**: Depending on your state or locality, you may need a specific license to transport waste, particularly if you handle hazardous materials. This license ensures that you are compliant with environmental laws concerning the safe transport and disposal of waste.
4. **Zoning Permits**: You'll need to ensure that your business complies with local zoning laws, which dictate where businesses can legally operate. If you plan to store equipment or vehicles, or handle waste sorting or recycling, your location needs to be zoned appropriately.
5. **Health and Safety Permits**: These are crucial if your business activities include handling potentially dangerous materials. Compliance with OSHA (Occupational Safety and Health Administration) and similar regulations is mandatory to protect the health and safety of your employees.

Steps to Acquire Licenses and Permits

Obtaining the necessary licenses and permits involves several **steps**, which include:

1. **Research**: Start by researching the specific requirements in your city and state. This information can often be found on official government

websites or by visiting local government offices.

2. **Prepare Documentation**: Gather all necessary documentation, which may include your business plan, proof of insurance, vehicle registration, and proof of identity and residency.
3. **Apply**: Fill out the necessary applications for each license and permit. This process may involve paying a fee, which can vary depending on the type and location of the permit.
4. **Inspections**: Some permits may require an inspection of your business premises or vehicles. Prepare for these inspections by ensuring that everything is compliant with the relevant regulations.
5. **Renewals**: Keep track of when each license and permit needs to be renewed. Operating with expired licenses can lead to the same penalties as operating without a license.

Managing Compliance

Once you have obtained all necessary licenses and permits, maintaining compliance is crucial. This involves:

- **Keeping Records**: Maintain up-to-date records of all licenses and permits, including copies of applications and renewal dates.
- **Staying Informed**: Laws and regulations can change. Stay informed about any changes that might affect your business by subscribing to relevant local government or industry newsletters.
- **Regular Reviews**: Conduct regular reviews of your business practices to ensure ongoing compliance. This can include periodic training sessions for your staff on relevant laws and safety practices.

Key Takeaways:

- **Legal Foundation**: Proper licensing and permits form the legal backbone of your junk removal business, enhancing credibility and operational security.

- **Continuous Compliance**: Managing your licenses and permits is an ongoing process that requires attention to detail and an understanding of local regulations.
- **Protect Your Business**: Compliance protects your business from fines and legal issues, and ensures the safety and health of your employees and the public.

By securing and managing the necessary licenses and permits, you are setting a strong foundation for the legal and successful operation of your junk removal business. As we move forward, we will delve into operational strategies that can enhance the efficiency and effectiveness of your services.

Chapter 3: Operational Strategies

Introduction to Chapter 3

Effective operational strategies are crucial for the success of any junk removal business. This chapter is dedicated to exploring various approaches to enhance your operations, ensuring not only efficiency but also safety and customer satisfaction. From route optimization to waste disposal best practices, each section is crafted to provide you with actionable insights that will improve your business operations.

3.1 Efficient Routing

Efficient routing is vital in the junk removal business, where time and fuel costs can significantly impact your bottom line. Effective route planning not only reduces operational costs but also allows you to serve more customers within the same time frame, enhancing profitability and customer satisfaction.

Benefits of Efficient Routing

1. **Reduced Fuel Costs**: By minimizing the distance traveled between jobs, you can significantly reduce fuel consumption, which is one of the major expenses in any logistics-based business.
2. **Increased Jobs Per Day**: Efficient routing allows you to fit more jobs into

a single day. This efficiency can lead to higher revenues without the need for additional resources.
3. **Lower Vehicle Wear and Tear**: Less time on the road means less wear and tear on your vehicles, reducing maintenance costs and extending the life of your fleet.
4. **Improved Customer Satisfaction**: Faster response times and predictable service windows lead to happier customers, enhancing your business's reputation and increasing the likelihood of repeat business and referrals.

Strategies for Route Optimization

- **Invest in GPS and Route Planning Software**: Modern GPS and routing software can dynamically create the most efficient routes based on real-time traffic conditions, job locations, and other variables. These tools are essential for maximizing operational efficiency.
- **Prioritize Jobs by Location**: Group jobs geographically to minimize travel time between stops. This can be done manually or with software that automatically schedules jobs based on their location relative to each other.
- **Flexible Scheduling**: Offer flexible scheduling options where possible. This allows you to adjust job timings based on other scheduled pickups in the same area, optimizing your daily routes.
- **Regular Route Reviews**: Continuously review and analyze the routes to identify any recurring issues or inefficiencies. This ongoing optimization can help you adapt to changes in traffic patterns, construction, and other factors that might impact your routes.

3.2 Waste Sorting and Disposal

Proper waste sorting and disposal are not only regulatory requirements but also critical to the sustainability and ethical standing of your business.

Effective waste management practices can also lead to cost savings and new revenue streams through recycling and resale of collectible items.

Benefits of Effective Waste Management

1. **Compliance with Regulations**: Adhering to local and federal waste disposal regulations prevents legal issues and fines.
2. **Environmental Responsibility**: Proper sorting and disposal minimize the environmental impact of your operations, aligning your business with growing consumer expectations for sustainability.
3. **Revenue from Recycled Materials**: Selling recyclable materials can become a significant revenue stream. Metals, electronics, and certain types of plastics have market value and can be sold to recycling companies.

Strategies for Effective Waste Management

- **Educate Your Team**: Conduct regular training sessions for your staff on the latest waste sorting techniques and disposal regulations. Knowledgeable employees are essential for compliance and efficiency.
- **Invest in the Right Tools**: Provide your team with the necessary tools for effective sorting—such as bins, labels, and protective gear. Consider investing in technology that can aid in the identification and sorting of recyclable materials.
- **Establish Partnerships with Recycling Centers**: Build relationships with local recycling centers and disposal facilities. Such partnerships can facilitate smoother operations and may provide financial benefits through preferred rates or services.
- **Monitor and Adjust Practices**: Regularly review and adjust your waste management practices based on new regulations, technological advances, and feedback from the team on the ground.

Key Takeaways:

- **Optimize Routes for Efficiency**: Utilize technology and strategic planning to ensure the most efficient use of resources.
- **Prioritize Compliance and Sustainability in Waste Management**: Adopt best practices in waste sorting and disposal to maintain regulatory compliance and support environmental sustainability.
- **Leverage Technology for Continuous Improvement**: Invest in systems and tools that enhance operational efficiency and waste management effectiveness.

In the next sections, we will explore additional operational strategies, including safety protocols and customer service excellence, further solidifying the foundation for a successful junk removal business.

3.3 Safety Protocols

Safety is paramount in the junk removal industry. The physical nature of the work, combined with the handling of potentially hazardous materials, demands rigorous safety protocols to protect both employees and customers. Implementing effective safety measures not only reduces the risk of accidents and injuries but also enhances your company's reputation as a responsible and trustworthy service provider.

Importance of Safety in Junk Removal

Operating a junk removal business involves inherent risks, including heavy lifting, exposure to hazardous substances, and the use of large vehicles. Accidents can lead to serious injuries, legal liabilities, and damage to your business's reputation. Therefore, prioritizing safety is not just a legal obligation—it's a critical business strategy.

Developing Comprehensive Safety Protocols

1. **Risk Assessment**: Conduct regular risk assessments to identify potential safety hazards associated with junk removal operations. This should include the evaluation of physical risks at job sites, potential hazards related to the materials being removed, and risks associated with the use of vehicles and equipment.
2. **Employee Training**: Provide comprehensive training for all employees on safety practices, including proper lifting techniques, the use of personal protective equipment (PPE), emergency procedures, and the handling of hazardous materials. Training should be ongoing and updated regularly to address new safety concerns or changes in regulations.
3. **Personal Protective Equipment (PPE)**: Ensure that all employees are equipped with the necessary PPE, which may include gloves, safety goggles, hard hats, and steel-toed boots. Regularly inspect PPE for wear and tear and replace it as needed.
4. **Vehicle Safety**: Implement strict protocols for vehicle operation and maintenance. This includes regular safety checks and servicing of all company vehicles to ensure they are safe and roadworthy. Additionally, train employees in safe driving practices, particularly focusing on the challenges of operating larger vehicles like trucks.
5. **Emergency Preparedness**: Develop and regularly update an emergency response plan. This plan should include procedures for dealing with accidents, injuries, hazardous material spills, and other emergencies. Ensure all employees are familiar with this plan and conduct regular drills to practice their response.
6. **Communication**: Maintain clear lines of communication across the organization. Encourage employees to report safety concerns and suggest improvements to safety protocols. Regular safety meetings can help reinforce the importance of safety and ensure everyone is informed about any changes or updates to safety procedures.

Benefits of Robust Safety Protocols

- **Reduced Workplace Injuries**: Effective safety protocols significantly reduce the likelihood of injuries, which can improve employee morale, reduce downtime, and minimize workers' compensation claims.
- **Compliance with Regulations**: Adhering to safety regulations helps avoid fines and legal actions that can arise from non-compliance.
- **Enhanced Reputation**: A strong commitment to safety demonstrates to customers and partners that your business is professional and reliable. This can be a competitive advantage in the marketplace.

Implementing and Monitoring Safety Protocols

- **Regular Audits and Reviews**: Conduct regular audits of safety protocols to ensure they are being followed and are effective. This includes revisiting risk assessments and training programs to ensure they are up-to-date with current best practices and regulations.
- **Feedback Loop**: Establish a feedback loop that allows employees to contribute to the ongoing improvement of safety practices. Worker input is invaluable as they are on the front lines and often have the best understanding of the risks and efficacy of current practices.
- **Investment in Safety**: Allocate sufficient resources to safety initiatives, including training, equipment, and health and safety management systems. Viewing safety spending as an investment rather than a cost can yield significant long-term benefits.

Key Takeaways:

- **Prioritize Employee Training**: Regular and comprehensive training is crucial for maintaining a safe work environment.
- **Invest in Proper Equipment**: Adequate safety equipment and well maintained vehicles are essential for preventing accidents.
- **Continuously Improve Safety Measures**: Regularly update and refine safety protocols to adapt to new challenges and ensure ongoing compliance with industry standards.

Safety is a critical aspect of every facet of operations in a junk removal business. Next, we will explore strategies for delivering excellent customer service, which is equally important for ensuring the success and growth of your business.

3.4 Customer Service Excellence

In the competitive junk removal industry, excellent customer service can distinguish your business from the rest. Providing top-notch service leads to higher customer satisfaction, increases repeat business, and enhances the likelihood of referrals. This section discusses strategies to ensure your junk removal service consistently delivers exceptional customer experiences.

Understanding Customer Expectations

The first step to excellent customer service is understanding what your customers expect from your junk removal service. Typically, they look for reliability, efficiency, courtesy, and transparency. Meeting these expectations can turn a one-time service into a lasting business relationship.

Strategies for Enhancing Customer Service

1. **Reliable Scheduling**: Ensure that your scheduling system is efficient and reliable. Use technology to manage appointments effectively and send reminders to customers about upcoming services. Being punctual shows respect for your customers' time and enhances your company's reputation.
2. **Transparent Pricing**: Customers appreciate transparency in pricing. Avoid hidden fees and provide clear, upfront estimates based on a detailed assessment of the job. This can be facilitated by using digital tools that allow customers to submit photos or descriptions for a more accurate

CHAPTER 3: OPERATIONAL STRATEGIES

quote.

3. **Professionalism**: Train your staff to be professional at all times. This includes wearing uniforms, being polite, and maintaining a positive attitude. The appearance and behavior of your staff reflect directly on your business and significantly impact customer perceptions.
4. **Effective Communication**: Keep customers informed throughout the service process. If delays or problems occur, communicate these promptly and honestly, along with the steps you're taking to resolve the issue. Good communication builds trust and reduces customer frustration.
5. **Quality Service**: Perform junk removal tasks meticulously. Ensure that the work area is clean and tidy once the job is done, and go the extra mile whenever possible. For example, offer to sweep the area after clearing out debris.
6. **Feedback Mechanism**: Implement a system to collect customer feedback regularly. This can be through follow-up calls, satisfaction surveys, or digital platforms. Use the feedback to continually improve your services.
7. **Handling Complaints**: Train your team on handling complaints effectively. Addressing customer concerns promptly and effectively can turn a potentially negative experience into a positive one, often enhancing customer loyalty.

Training and Empowerment

Empowering your employees is key to delivering excellent customer service. When your team feels confident and supported, they are more likely to exceed customer expectations.

- **Training Programs**: Regularly train your team on customer service best practices, including how to interact with customers, manage their time, handle disputes, and perform their tasks efficiently and safely.
- **Empowerment**: Allow your employees some autonomy to make decisions on the spot, particularly when it comes to resolving customer issues. Empowerment can lead to quicker resolution of problems, enhancing

customer satisfaction.
- **Recognition**: Recognize and reward employees who go above and beyond in their customer service efforts. Recognition not only boosts morale but also encourages other team members to improve their service.

Leveraging Technology

Technology can greatly enhance the customer service aspect of your junk removal business:

- **CRM Systems**: Use Customer Relationship Management (CRM) systems to maintain detailed records of customer interactions, preferences, and feedback. This information can be invaluable for personalizing service and resolving any issues effectively.
- **Mobile Apps**: Consider developing a mobile app that allows customers to book services, view their service history, and communicate directly with your company. Apps can provide convenience and improve overall customer engagement.
- **Social Media**: Utilize social media platforms to engage with customers, promote your services, and provide quick customer service. Active social media presence helps keep your business top of mind and enhances your accessibility.

Key Takeaways:

- **Customer-Centric Approach**: Always prioritize the needs and satisfaction of your customers.
- **Continuous Improvement**: Regularly seek ways to enhance the customer service aspect of your business based on direct feedback from your clients.
- **Invest in People and Technology**: Support your customer service strategies with the right training and technology to maximize efficiency and effectiveness.

By focusing on these customer service strategies, your junk removal business can build a strong reputation for reliability and quality, setting the stage for growth and success in a competitive market.

Chapter 4: Marketing and Customer Acquisition

Introduction to Chapter 4

In the junk removal industry, effective marketing and strategic customer acquisition are essential to driving growth and building a sustainable business. This chapter focuses on crafting a marketing strategy that not only attracts new customers but also nurtures existing relationships, ensuring a steady stream of business through various channels. From digital strategies to grassroots marketing, we'll explore diverse tactics that can enhance your visibility and appeal in a competitive market.

4.1 Digital Marketing Strategies

In today's digital age, having a strong online presence is crucial for any business, including junk removal services. Effective digital marketing strategies can help you reach a broader audience, engage potential customers, and convert leads into bookings.

Key Components of Digital Marketing

1. **Website Development**: Your website is often the first point of contact

between your business and potential customers. It should be professionally designed, easy to navigate, and optimized for search engines (SEO). Include essential information such as services offered, pricing, contact details, and a simple booking form.

2. **Search Engine Optimization (SEO)**: Optimize your website with relevant keywords, quality content, and meta tags to ensure it ranks high in search engine results. Local SEO is particularly important for junk removal services to target customers in specific geographic areas.

3. **Content Marketing**: Create and share valuable content related to junk removal. This could include blog posts on decluttering tips, recycling guidelines, or the environmental benefits of proper waste disposal. Content marketing can establish your brand as a thought leader and attract organic traffic to your site.

4. **Social Media Marketing**: Utilize platforms like Facebook, Instagram, and Twitter to connect with customers. Post before-and-after photos of your work, share customer testimonials, and run targeted ads to increase engagement and reach.

5. **Email Marketing**: Build an email list and engage with your audience through regular newsletters and exclusive offers. Email marketing helps keep your brand top-of-mind and can encourage repeat business.

Strategies for Effective Digital Marketing

- **Track and Measure**: Use analytics to track the effectiveness of your digital marketing efforts. Tools like Google Analytics can provide insights into website traffic, user behavior, and conversion rates, helping you refine your strategies.
- **Engage and Interact**: Actively engage with your audience online. Respond to comments, answer queries, and participate in relevant online communities. Engagement increases trust and loyalty among potential customers.
- **Adapt and Evolve**: Digital marketing trends are constantly changing. Stay updated with the latest technologies and platforms, and be prepared to

adapt your strategies to maintain a competitive edge.

4.2 Branding Your Business

Strong branding differentiates your junk removal service from competitors and creates a memorable impression on consumers. Branding goes beyond just a logo or a tagline; it encompasses the customer's entire experience with your company.

Elements of Strong Branding

1. **Brand Identity**: Develop a unique brand identity that includes a logo, color scheme, and a consistent theme across all marketing materials. This identity should reflect your business's values and appeal to your target audience.
2. **Brand Voice**: Establish a brand voice that resonates with your audience. Whether professional, friendly, or humorous, your communication should be consistent in tone and reflect your brand personality.
3. **Brand Promise**: Clearly communicate what your brand stands for. Whether it's reliability, fast service, or eco-friendliness, your brand promise should align with your customer's expectations and your company's values.

Strategies for Building a Strong Brand

- **Consistency is Key**: Ensure that all your marketing materials, from your website to your vehicle signage, consistently reflect your brand identity and values. This consistency helps reinforce your brand image and aids in customer recall.
- **Leverage Testimonials and Reviews**: Positive reviews and testimonials

can be powerful tools for building trust and credibility. Encourage satisfied customers to leave reviews online, and feature these testimonials prominently on your website and social media.
- **Community Involvement**: Participate in community events and support local causes. This not only boosts your brand visibility but also establishes your business as a responsible and integral part of the community.

Key Takeaways:

- **Invest in Digital Presence**: A robust online presence is essential to attract and engage today's consumers.
- **Emphasize Branding**: Strong branding sets your business apart and can influence a customer's decision to choose your service over others.
- **Continuous Engagement**: Regularly interacting with customers and the community enhances brand loyalty and aids in long-term business growth.

By integrating these marketing and branding strategies, your junk removal business can attract new customers, create meaningful engagements, and establish a strong market presence. In the next section, we will delve into networking and partnership strategies to further expand your reach and influence in the market.

4.3 Networking and Partnerships

For a junk removal business, building a network and establishing partnerships can be transformative, enhancing both your operational capabilities and market reach. Networking not only connects you with potential clients but also with other businesses and community leaders who can provide referrals and collaboration opportunities. Effective partnerships can lead to a broader service offering and access to new customer bases.

Benefits of Networking and Building Partnerships

1. **Referrals**: Strong professional relationships can lead to referrals, which are often a reliable source of new business. Happy clients and connected business partners who trust your services are more likely to recommend your business to others.
2. **Increased Business Opportunities**: Partnerships with property management companies, real estate agents, and construction firms can open up steady streams of business. These companies often require junk removal services regularly and can provide consistent contracts.
3. **Resource Sharing**: Networking can lead to opportunities for sharing resources, such as marketing costs or operational tools, reducing expenses and enhancing business capabilities.
4. **Enhanced Community Presence**: Being active in local business networks and community groups can raise your business's profile and build its reputation within the community.

Strategies for Effective Networking and Partnership Building

- **Join Local Business Associations**: Engage with local chambers of commerce, trade groups, or professional associations. These groups often provide networking opportunities, business resources, and community exposure.
- **Attend Industry Conferences and Events**: Participate in industry-related events, workshops, and conferences. These can be excellent venues to meet potential partners, learn about industry trends, and expose your brand to a broader audience.
- **Leverage Online Platforms**: Utilize LinkedIn and other professional social networks to connect with other business owners and potential partners. Regularly update your profiles and engage with others' content to increase visibility.
- **Offer Co-Marketing Opportunities**: Propose co-marketing ventures with businesses that offer complementary services, such as moving companies

or estate sale organizers. This could involve joint advertising campaigns or bundled service offerings.
- **Develop Community Projects**: Initiate or participate in community projects or charity events. These initiatives can improve your business's visibility and foster goodwill within the community, making your business a known and trusted entity.

Crafting a Partnership Proposal

When approaching a potential partner, it's important to have a clear and professional proposal that outlines the benefits of the partnership for both parties.

1. **Identify Potential Partners**: Look for businesses that are aligned with your services and whose customers might require junk removal. These could include renovation companies, storage facilities, or home and garden businesses.
2. **Outline Mutual Benefits**: Clearly state how the partnership can benefit both parties. For instance, you could offer a referral fee for any business sent your way or provide enhanced service options for the partner's customers.
3. **Propose Specific Ideas**: Include specific ideas for how the partnership could work, such as joint promotional events, shared branding on marketing materials, or exclusive discounts for referrals.
4. **Follow Up**: After presenting your proposal, be sure to follow up. Maintain regular contact to keep your business top of mind and to nurture the relationship.

Key Takeaways:

- **Proactive Relationship Building**: Actively seek out and cultivate relationships within your business community.
- **Mutually Beneficial Arrangements**: Focus on creating partnerships that

offer clear benefits to all involved parties, enhancing the chances of long-term success.
- **Community Engagement**: Regular involvement in community events and initiatives can significantly boost your business's local profile and credibility.

By integrating robust networking and partnership strategies, your junk removal business can expand its reach, build its reputation, and secure a more stable and profitable operational base. In the next section, we will explore strategies to retain customers, ensuring ongoing business success through repeat bookings and customer loyalty.

4.4 Retention Strategies

While acquiring new customers is crucial for the growth of your junk removal business, retaining existing customers can be even more beneficial. Customer retention strategies lead to increased profitability as the cost of retaining an existing customer is significantly lower than acquiring a new one. Loyal customers also tend to buy more over time and can become advocates for your brand, referring new clients through word-of-mouth. This section explores effective strategies to enhance customer loyalty and encourage repeat business.

Understanding Customer Retention

Customer retention refers to your ability to keep your current customers engaged and committed to your services over time. It involves providing ongoing value that meets or exceeds the expectations set during their initial interaction with your business. Effective retention strategies can significantly impact your business's bottom line by stabilizing revenue and reducing the volatility associated with constantly acquiring new customers.

CHAPTER 4: MARKETING AND CUSTOMER ACQUISITION

Strategies for Enhancing Customer Retention

1. **Exceptional Customer Service**: Consistently delivering outstanding customer service is the cornerstone of customer retention. Ensure that every customer interaction is positive, professional, and focused on meeting the customer's needs. This includes everything from the initial contact and timely removal services to courteous follow-up communication.
2. **Quality of Service Delivery**: Ensure that the quality of your junk removal service is excellent every time. This means being punctual, thorough, and respectful of the customer's property. Leaving a site cleaner than when you arrived can make a lasting impression and increase the likelihood of repeat business.
3. **Loyalty Programs**: Implement loyalty programs that reward repeat customers. This could be in the form of discounts, special promotions, or access to exclusive services. Loyalty programs not only encourage repeat business but also enhance customer engagement and satisfaction.
4. **Regular Communication**: Keep in touch with your customers through regular updates via emails, newsletters, or text messages. Use these communications to inform them about new services, special promotions, or helpful tips related to junk removal. Regular, value-added communication keeps your brand top of mind without being overly sales-focused.
5. **Feedback and Continuous Improvement**: Actively seek customer feedback to understand their needs and how well your service meets their expectations. This can be done through surveys, direct calls, or digital feedback forms. Use this feedback to continuously improve your service offerings. Showing customers that their input has led to tangible changes can significantly boost loyalty.
6. **Personalization**: Tailor your communications and services to meet individual customer needs. Use the data you've collected about your customers to personalize your interactions, such as acknowledging special occasions like anniversaries or offering services tailored to their past preferences.

7. **Problem Resolution**: Handle customer complaints and issues promptly and effectively. A well-handled complaint can often convert a dissatisfied customer into a loyal one. Ensure your staff is trained in effective complaint resolution strategies and empowered to make decisions that prioritize customer satisfaction.

Implementing Effective Retention Tactics

- **Integrate Technology**: Utilize CRM (Customer Relationship Management) systems to manage customer data, track interactions, and personalize communication. Technology can streamline these processes and ensure no customer feels neglected.
- **Educate Your Team**: Regular training sessions for your team on the importance of customer retention and how to execute retention strategies effectively can enhance their performance and, consequently, customer satisfaction.
- **Monitor Retention Metrics**: Keep track of key performance indicators (KPIs) related to customer retention, such as repeat customer rate, customer lifetime value, and net promoter score (NPS). These metrics will help you gauge the effectiveness of your retention strategies and identify areas for improvement.

Key Takeaways:

- **Focus on Long-Term Relationships**: View each customer interaction as part of an ongoing relationship, rather than a one-time transaction.
- **Invest in Loyalty**: Develop loyalty programs that add value to the customer experience and encourage ongoing engagement.
- **Leverage Feedback**: Use customer feedback as a tool for continuous service improvement, thereby reinforcing the value placed on customer opinions.

By implementing these retention strategies, your junk removal business can cultivate a loyal customer base that not only contributes to steady revenue growth but also enhances your reputation through positive word-of-mouth. This stable customer base will serve as a foundation for sustained success as you continue to explore new growth opportunities in the market.

Chapter 5: Niche Opportunities in Junk Removal

Introduction to Chapter 5

Diversifying your service offerings can significantly enhance the growth potential of your junk removal business. By tapping into niche markets within the broader junk removal industry, you can cater to specific customer needs, reduce competition, and increase your company's revenue streams. This chapter explores various niche opportunities that can set your business apart and appeal to a wider range of clients.

5.1 E-Waste Management

Electronic waste, or e-waste, is one of the fastest-growing waste streams globally, fueled by the rapid pace of technological innovation and shortening lifespans of electronic devices. Managing e-waste presents a unique challenge due to the hazardous materials often contained in electronics, which require special handling and disposal processes.

Opportunities in E-Waste Management

1. **Growing Demand**: The increasing volume of e-waste generates a demand for specialized removal and recycling services. Providing these services can tap into a market with significant growth potential.
2. **Regulatory Compliance**: Many regions have strict regulations governing the disposal of e-waste, creating a need for compliant removal services that can navigate these legal complexities.
3. **Value Recovery**: E-waste contains valuable materials like gold, silver, and copper, which can be recovered and sold. Developing capabilities to refine and sell these materials can open additional revenue streams.

Strategies for Capturing the E-Waste Market

- **Certification and Training**: Obtain certifications related to e-waste handling and disposal to build credibility and ensure compliance with environmental regulations.
- **Partner with Recyclers**: Establish partnerships with certified e-waste recyclers. These partnerships can provide streamlined pathways for processing and disposing of collected e-waste.
- **Public Education**: Engage in public education campaigns about the importance of proper e-waste disposal. Educating the public can increase the demand for your services and position your business as a thought leader in the industry.

5.2 Estate Cleanouts

Estate cleanouts involve clearing out properties after a death or significant transition, such as downsizing for elderly individuals. These projects can be large-scale and emotionally charged, requiring a sensitive and efficient approach.

Opportunities in Estate Cleanouts

1. **High-Value Contracts**: Estate cleanouts can be extensive and involve valuable items that need careful handling or can be sold or donated, providing opportunities for additional revenue.
2. **Service Expansion**: Offering comprehensive services, including the valuation and sale of items, cleaning, and preparing properties for sale, can differentiate your business in the marketplace.

Strategies for Developing Estate Cleanout Services

- **Build Relationships with Estate Lawyers and Realtors**: Networking with professionals who regularly handle estates can lead to referrals and steady business opportunities.
- **Training in Valuation and Handling**: Train your staff in appraising items and handling them with care. This expertise can be a key selling point for your services.
- **Sensitive Marketing Approach**: Tailor your marketing materials to address the emotional aspects of estate cleanouts, emphasizing respect, dignity, and professionalism.

5.3 Commercial Contracts

Securing commercial contracts for regular junk removal from businesses like offices, retail stores, and industrial sites can provide stable, long-term income. These contracts are typically larger and more predictable than individual residential jobs.

Opportunities in Commercial Contracts

1. **Steady Work**: Commercial entities often generate consistent waste

streams that require regular management.
2. **Larger Scale Contracts**: Commercial jobs are usually larger than residential ones, potentially leading to higher revenue per job.

Strategies for Securing Commercial Contracts

- **Targeted Marketing**: Develop marketing campaigns that specifically address the needs of business clients, such as reliability, cost-effectiveness, and compliance with waste disposal laws.
- **Customized Service Plans**: Offer flexible and tailored service plans that can adapt to the specific needs of commercial clients, such as after-hours service to minimize disruption to their operations.
- **Professionalism and Reliability**: Maintain high standards of professionalism and reliability, as these are critical factors for business clients.

Key Takeaways:

- **Explore Niche Markets**: Diversifying into niche areas like e-waste management, estate cleanouts, and commercial contracts can reduce competition and increase profitability.
- **Tailor Strategies to Target Markets**: Develop specialized marketing and operational strategies that cater to the specific needs of each niche market.
- **Leverage Expertise and Relationships**: Build expertise in your chosen niches and cultivate relationships with key stakeholders and potential referral sources.

By exploring these niche opportunities, your junk removal business can expand its services, meet diverse client needs, and build a reputation for excellence in specialized areas of junk removal. In the next sections, we will continue to explore other potential areas for diversification and growth within the industry.

5.4 Specialty Items Disposal

Disposing of specialty items presents a unique set of challenges and opportunities within the junk removal industry. These items can include anything from pianos and large furniture to hazardous materials and construction debris. Each category requires specific handling, disposal methods, or recycling processes that adhere to local regulations, providing a niche service where your business can excel.

Opportunities in Specialty Items Disposal

1. **High Demand for Expertise**: Many items cannot be disposed of through regular waste services due to their size, material, or potential environmental hazards. Providing specialized disposal services can position your business as an expert in this niche market.
2. **Premium Pricing**: Specialty disposal often allows for premium pricing due to the expertise and additional effort required. This can significantly increase your profit margins.
3. **Partnerships with Retailers and Manufacturers**: Establishing relationships with furniture stores, home appliance retailers, and construction companies can lead to regular referral business as these partners often need reliable disposal services for their customers.

Strategies for Capitalizing on Specialty Items Disposal

- **Invest in Training and Equipment**: Ensure your team is well-trained and equipped to handle various types of specialty items. This might include training for safe handling and transportation of heavy items, or the proper methods for disposing of hazardous materials.
- **Certification and Compliance**: Obtain necessary certifications and ensure compliance with all relevant environmental and safety regulations. This not only protects your business legally but also builds trust with your

customers.
- **Marketing Expertise**: Highlight your capability to handle complex disposal challenges in your marketing materials. Use case studies or testimonials that showcase your expertise and reliability in handling specialty items.
- **Streamlined Logistics**: Develop efficient logistics to handle the collection, transportation, and disposal of bulky or hazardous items. This may include investing in specialized equipment or vehicles designed to manage these types of materials safely.

5.5 Building Partnerships in Specialty Disposal

Establishing strategic partnerships can enhance your capacity to handle specialty disposals effectively:

- **Waste Processing Facilities**: Build relationships with local waste processing and recycling facilities. Understand their capabilities and limitations so you can assure clients that their items are disposed of responsibly.
- **Local Government Contracts**: Many municipalities outsource the disposal of specialty items to private companies. Securing government contracts can provide a steady flow of business.
- **Event-Based Opportunities**: Offer your services for events like home and garden shows, trade fairs, or local clean-up days. These events can provide opportunities to raise awareness of your specialty disposal services and gain new customers.

Challenges in Specialty Items Disposal

- **Regulatory Hurdles**: Disposing of hazardous materials or large items often involves navigating complex regulations that can vary significantly

by locality.
- **High Operational Costs**: The equipment, transportation, and disposal costs associated with specialty items can be substantial. Effective cost management is crucial to maintain profitability.
- **Customer Education**: Customers may not be aware of the complexities involved in disposing of certain items. Educating them about the value of your service is essential to justify your pricing and the necessity of specialty disposal.

Key Takeaways:

- **Specialize and Certify**: Gain the necessary certifications and focus on areas that require specific expertise, setting your business apart as a specialist in the field.
- **Market Strategically**: Use targeted marketing to educate and attract customers who specifically need specialty item disposal services.
- **Manage Costs and Compliance**: Keep a tight rein on operational costs and stay compliant with all regulations to ensure your specialty disposal services are both profitable and sustainable.

By integrating specialty items disposal into your service offerings, you not only meet a critical market need but also enhance your business's overall value proposition. This niche service can attract a diverse clientele, from residential customers to large corporations and government agencies, all looking for expert handling of complex disposal challenges. In the next section, we will explore the role of technology in optimizing and expanding your junk removal services, further enhancing your business's efficiency and competitive edge.

Chapter 6: Technology in Junk Removal

Introduction to Chapter 6

In the modern era, technology plays a pivotal role in transforming traditional business operations across various industries, including junk removal. Leveraging technology not only enhances operational efficiency but also improves customer service, safety, and environmental compliance. This chapter delves into how integrating advanced technologies can drive innovation, streamline processes, and create a competitive advantage for your junk removal business.

6.1 Software Solutions

Implementing the right software solutions can significantly streamline your junk removal business's operations, from scheduling and routing to customer management and invoicing. Here's a look at key types of software that can elevate your business:

Types of Software Solutions

1. **Customer Relationship Management (CRM) Software**: This tool helps manage your interactions with current and potential customers. CRM systems can track customer activity, manage leads, automate marketing communications, and organize customer service efforts, making them

essential for maintaining strong customer relationships.
2. **Route Optimization Software**: This technology uses algorithms to determine the most efficient routes for daily jobs. It takes into account various factors such as traffic conditions, job location, vehicle capacity, and customer time preferences, thereby reducing fuel costs and improving service times.
3. **Inventory and Equipment Management Software**: Keep track of your equipment and vehicles with software that monitors usage, maintenance schedules, and even depreciation. This helps in managing operational costs and planning for future investments.
4. **Financial Software**: Tools like QuickBooks or Xero can help manage your finances, from invoicing and payroll to taxes and revenue tracking. Integrating financial software ensures accuracy in your financial dealings and provides valuable insights into your business's economic health.

Benefits of Implementing Software Solutions

- **Efficiency and Time Savings**: Automation of routine tasks frees up your time and resources, allowing you to focus on growing your business.
- **Enhanced Customer Satisfaction**: Software that enhances scheduling, communication, and job tracking leads to better customer service, increasing satisfaction and loyalty.
- **Data-Driven Decisions**: These systems provide valuable data that can be analyzed to make informed decisions about marketing, service improvements, and business growth strategies.

6.2 Automating Your Operations

Automation in the junk removal industry can significantly enhance operational efficiency and employee productivity. Here's how you can automate various aspects of your operations:

Areas for Automation

1. **Job Scheduling and Dispatch**: Automated scheduling tools ensure that jobs are booked without conflicts and that the nearest and most appropriate crews are dispatched, improving response times and operational efficiency.
2. **Customer Communications**: Automated emails or text messages for appointment confirmations, reminders, and follow-ups can improve customer engagement and reduce no-shows.
3. **Payment Processing**: Automate your billing and payment collections to reduce the administrative burden and improve cash flow. Online payment solutions can integrate seamlessly into your service offerings, providing convenience for your customers.

Implementing Automation in Your Business

- **Identify Repetitive Tasks**: Start by identifying tasks that are repetitive and time-consuming. These are prime candidates for automation.
- **Choose the Right Tools**: Select software that integrates well with your existing systems and meets your specific needs. Consider factors like cost, scalability, user-friendliness, and customer support.
- **Train Your Team**: Ensure your team is well-trained on any new technology. This will maximize its effectiveness and ensure smooth integration into your daily operations.

6.3 Using Technology for Competitive Advantage

In a competitive market, technology can be a significant differentiator. Here's how you can use technology to set your business apart:

Innovative Uses of Technology

1. **Mobile Apps**: Develop a custom mobile app that allows customers to easily book services, track the status of their job, and even make payments. An app can enhance the customer experience and improve engagement.
2. **Eco-Friendly Technology**: Utilize technology that helps reduce your environmental impact, such as electric vehicles or solar-powered equipment. Promote these initiatives to attract environmentally conscious consumers.
3. **Virtual Estimations**: Implement technology that allows virtual job estimations through customer-submitted videos or photos, reducing the need for on-site estimates and saving time for both the customer and your team.

Key Takeaways:

- **Embrace Digital Transformation**: Leveraging technology can streamline your operations, enhance customer service, and provide valuable insights through data analytics.
- **Invest in the Right Tools**: Select technologies that align with your business goals and scale with your growth.
- **Market Your Innovations**: Use your technological advancements as marketing points to differentiate your business in the market.

By integrating advanced technologies into your junk removal business, you can improve operational efficiencies, enhance customer satisfaction, and ultimately position your business as a leader in the industry. In the next sections, we will explore further operational strategies that can complement these technological advancements.

6.4 Using Technology for Competitive Advantage

In the competitive world of junk removal, leveraging technology can significantly enhance your company's ability to stand out, offering efficiencies and services that set you apart from the competition. This section delves into various technological advancements that can not only streamline operations but also create unique selling propositions that attract more customers.

Innovative Technological Tools

Adopting cutting-edge tools and technologies can transform the way your business operates, providing a better customer experience and improving operational efficiencies:

1. **Advanced Analytics for Business Insights**: Utilize data analytics platforms to gain deep insights into your business operations. These tools can analyze patterns in customer behavior, operational efficiency, and even route optimization, providing actionable insights that can lead to better decision-making.
2. **Automated Customer Service Solutions**: Implement chatbots and AI-driven customer service solutions on your website and social media platforms. These tools can provide instant responses to customer inquiries, book appointments, and even handle basic customer service tasks, enhancing the customer experience and freeing up your staff for more complex issues.
3. **Internet of Things (IoT) for Fleet Management**: Equip your vehicles

with IoT devices that can track vehicle locations, monitor fuel usage, and manage maintenance schedules in real time. This technology not only improves the efficiency of your operations but also helps in reducing costs and enhancing the reliability of your services.

Enhancing Customer Experience with Technology

Technology can play a crucial role in differentiating your service offerings by enhancing the customer experience:

1. **Mobile App Functionality**: Develop a comprehensive mobile app that allows customers to schedule pickups, track the progress of their junk removal, and communicate directly with your team. Features like in-app payments and digital receipts can add convenience and transparency to the customer experience.
2. **Virtual Reality (VR) Estimations**: Incorporate VR technology to provide virtual estimations to your customers. Through VR, customers can show your team the items they need removed without an on-site visit, providing convenience and a novel experience.
3. **Personalized Service Offerings**: Use technology to offer personalized services based on customer preferences and previous interactions. Machine learning algorithms can help tailor your marketing efforts and service offerings to individual customer needs, increasing satisfaction and loyalty.

Operational Efficiency Through Technology

Streamlining operations using technology not only reduces costs but also increases your business's capacity to handle more jobs efficiently:

1. **Dynamic Scheduling Systems**: Implement dynamic scheduling systems that automatically adjust your job schedules based on real-time data such as traffic conditions, job duration, and customer preferences. This

flexibility can improve efficiency and customer satisfaction.
2. **Robotic Process Automation (RPA)**: Use RPA to automate routine administrative tasks such as billing, payroll, and compliance checks. Automation reduces the likelihood of human error and allows your team to focus on more strategic activities.
3. **Eco-Friendly Technological Solutions**: Adopt green technologies such as electric vehicles and solar-powered equipment. Not only do these technologies reduce your carbon footprint, but they also appeal to environmentally conscious consumers, providing a market advantage.

Strategic Implementation of Technology

Successfully integrating technology into your business involves strategic planning and consideration:

- **Evaluate Technology Needs**: Assess which areas of your business would benefit most from technological upgrades. Consider both customer-facing and operational aspects.
- **Staff Training and Adoption**: Ensure that your team is properly trained on new technologies. Adoption can be a challenge, and it's crucial that all team members are comfortable and proficient with the new tools.
- **Continuous Monitoring and Feedback**: Regularly monitor the performance of implemented technologies and solicit feedback from both customers and staff. Use this feedback to make adjustments and improve the technology's effectiveness.

Key Takeaways:

- **Leverage Technology for Differentiation**: Use technology not just for efficiency but also as a key differentiator in the market.
- **Focus on Customer Experience**: Enhance the customer journey through innovative technological solutions that add value and convenience.
- **Adopt Sustainable Practices**: Invest in eco-friendly technologies that not

only help the environment but also appeal to a growing segment of the market.

By strategically using technology, your junk removal business can achieve significant competitive advantages, creating a more efficient, customer-friendly, and innovative service offering. In the next chapter, we will explore how to scale these technological integrations as your business grows, ensuring that your technological infrastructure supports and enhances your expansion efforts.

Chapter 7: Scaling Your Business

Introduction to Chapter 7

Scaling a junk removal business involves expanding its capacity and operations to meet increased demand without compromising on service quality. It is a crucial phase that requires careful planning and strategic decision-making. This chapter outlines how to effectively scale your junk removal business, focusing on expanding services, exploring franchising options, enhancing team capabilities, and managing the challenges that come with growth.

7.1 Expanding Your Services

One of the key strategies for scaling your business is to broaden the range of services offered. This not only helps capture a larger market share but also diversifies revenue streams, which can stabilize your business during economic fluctuations.

Strategies for Service Expansion

1. **Identify Market Needs**: Conduct market research to identify unmet needs within your community. For instance, if there is a high demand for eco-friendly disposal solutions that are not adequately served, this could be a niche for your business.

2. **Develop Related Services**: Consider services that complement your existing offerings. If you're already doing residential junk removal, you might add estate cleanouts, recycling services, or document shredding services.
3. **Leverage Technology**: Use technology to add value to your services. For example, offering a customer portal for scheduling and payment can enhance the customer experience and set you apart from competitors.
4. **Partner with Other Businesses**: Form strategic partnerships with companies in related industries, such as moving companies or property management firms, to offer bundled services. This can increase the value provided to customers while also expanding your customer base.

7.2 Franchising Your Business

Franchising can be an effective way to expand your business's reach and brand without bearing the full cost of opening new locations. It involves allowing other entrepreneurs to open and operate branches of your business in different locations under your brand name.

Steps to Franchise Your Business

1. **Develop a Franchise Model**: Create a comprehensive business model that can be replicated. This includes standardized operating procedures, branding guidelines, and training programs.
2. **Legal Considerations**: Consult with a lawyer to draft a franchise agreement and ensure compliance with all relevant laws and regulations.
3. **Choose the Right Franchisees**: Select franchisees who are a good fit for your business culture and who have the necessary skills and motivation to succeed.
4. **Support Your Franchisees**: Provide ongoing support to your franchisees

to ensure they are successful. This can include training, marketing assistance, and regular business reviews.

7.3 Multi-location Expansion

Expanding to new locations can significantly increase your business's market presence and profitability. However, managing multiple locations presents unique challenges.

Strategies for Multi-location Expansion

1. **Market Research**: Before expanding to a new area, conduct thorough market research to ensure there is sufficient demand and that the market dynamics are favorable.
2. **Standardize Operations**: Create standardized operating procedures to ensure consistency in service quality across all locations. This helps maintain your brand's reputation.
3. **Manage Logistically**: Invest in logistics and supply chain management to ensure efficient operations across all locations. Consider centralized management systems to streamline operations.
4. **Local Management**: Employ local managers who understand the regional market and can make day-to-day decisions that align with corporate strategies.

7.4 Building a Team

As your business grows, so too does your need for a skilled and reliable team. Scaling effectively requires not only increasing the number of employees but also enhancing their skills and engagement.

Effective Team Expansion Strategies

1. **Structured Hiring Process**: Develop a structured recruitment process that helps you identify individuals who not only have the necessary skills but also fit well with your company culture.
2. **Training Programs**: Implement comprehensive training programs that help new hires understand your business operations and service standards.
3. **Employee Development**: Invest in your employees' professional development. Encourage and support them in pursuing certifications or further education that can benefit their roles.
4. **Employee Retention**: Focus on retaining top talent by fostering a positive work environment, offering competitive compensation packages, and recognizing and rewarding outstanding performance.

Key Takeaways:

- **Careful Planning**: Effective scaling requires careful strategic planning and a clear understanding of your business's goals and the market environment.
- **Invest in Infrastructure**: Ensure that your business infrastructure, including technology and human resources, can support your growth ambitions.
- **Monitor and Adapt**: Continuously monitor the performance of all areas of your business as you scale, and be prepared to make adjustments as necessary.

Scaling your junk removal business involves a delicate balance of expanding your service offerings, exploring new markets, franchising, and building a capable team. With careful planning and execution, you can successfully grow your business while maintaining high service standards and profitability. In the next chapter, we will explore sustainability practices that can further enhance your business's reputation and appeal in a competitive market.

Chapter 8: Sustainability Practices

Introduction to Chapter 8

In today's environmentally conscious market, adopting sustainable practices is not only beneficial for the planet but also advantageous for business growth and reputation. A junk removal business that emphasizes sustainability can differentiate itself from competitors and attract customers who value ecological responsibility. This chapter discusses various sustainability practices that can be integrated into your junk removal business to enhance its environmental and social impact.

8.1 Recycling Initiatives

Recycling is a cornerstone of sustainable waste management. By implementing robust recycling initiatives, your business can significantly reduce the amount of waste sent to landfills and potentially tap into new revenue streams through the sale of recyclable materials.

Strategies for Enhancing Recycling Efforts

1. **Comprehensive Sorting Systems**: Invest in training and equipment to ensure that recyclable materials are properly sorted at the point of collection. This may involve the use of specialized sorting facilities or

on-site sorting processes.
2. **Educate Your Customers**: Provide customers with clear information about what can and cannot be recycled. Education can increase recycling rates and improve the quality of recyclable materials collected, reducing contamination.
3. **Partner with Recycling Centers**: Develop partnerships with local recycling centers to ensure that materials are processed responsibly and efficiently. These partnerships can also provide economic benefits if you can negotiate favorable terms for the sale of recyclable commodities.
4. **Track and Report**: Implement systems to track the volume and types of materials recycled. Reporting these figures can not only help with operational efficiency but also serve as a marketing tool to attract environmentally conscious customers.

8.2 Partnering with Environmental Organizations

Collaborating with environmental organizations can enhance your business's credibility and impact. These partnerships can range from participating in community clean-up events to supporting environmental advocacy initiatives.

Benefits of Environmental Partnerships

1. **Enhanced Brand Image**: Association with respected environmental organizations can enhance your brand's reputation and appeal to a broader customer base.
2. **Community Engagement**: Participating in environmental programs can increase your visibility and engagement within the community, building goodwill and customer loyalty.
3. **Shared Knowledge and Resources**: Partnerships can provide access to additional resources and expertise, helping your business improve its

environmental practices.

Strategies for Building Environmental Partnerships

- **Identify Alignment**: Look for organizations whose missions align with your business values. This alignment ensures that the partnership is mutually beneficial and sustainable.
- **Engage Actively**: Don't just donate money; actively participate in events and initiatives. This hands-on involvement can be more rewarding and impactful for your team and community.
- **Promote Jointly**: Use your marketing channels to promote your environmental partnerships and initiatives. This not only raises awareness for the cause but also demonstrates your commitment to environmental responsibility.

8.3 Reducing Carbon Footprint

Reducing your carbon footprint is crucial for minimizing your business's environmental impact. Implementing practices to reduce emissions can also lead to cost savings, particularly in fuel and energy consumption.

Carbon Reduction Strategies

1. **Fuel-Efficient Vehicles**: Invest in fuel-efficient or electric vehicles for your fleet. These vehicles can reduce emissions and lower fuel costs over time.
2. **Route Optimization**: Use route optimization software to minimize driving distances and reduce fuel consumption.
3. **Energy-Efficient Operations**: Implement energy-saving measures in your facilities, such as using LED lighting, energy-efficient appliances,

and smart thermostats.

8.4 Community Involvement

Engaging with the community is not only a way to build brand loyalty but also to reinforce your commitment to sustainability. Initiatives can include local clean-ups, educational programs, and support for local environmental projects.

Benefits of Community Involvement

1. **Building Relationships**: Strong community ties can lead to increased business opportunities and customer loyalty.
2. **Enhancing Employee Morale**: Employees often feel more connected and motivated when their company actively contributes to the community.

Strategies for Effective Community Engagement

- **Organize Events**: Host or sponsor local environmental events that encourage community participation.
- **Volunteer Programs**: Develop a volunteer program that allows employees to participate in community service during work hours.
- **Educational Outreach**: Offer educational programs in schools or community centers to teach about waste reduction and recycling.

Key Takeaways:

- **Integrate Sustainability**: Make sustainability a core part of your business model, not just an add-on.
- **Leverage Technology and Partnerships**: Use technology to reduce waste

and partner with organizations that can enhance your sustainability efforts.
- **Communicate Your Efforts**: Actively communicate your sustainability practices to customers, not only to inform them but also to encourage their participation.

By adopting and promoting sustainable practices, your junk removal business can play a crucial role in environmental conservation, while also building a stronger, more respected brand that attracts a loyal customer base. In the next chapter, we will explore financial management strategies to ensure the economic sustainability of your business as you implement these environmentally friendly practices.

Chapter 9: Financial Management

Introduction to Chapter 9

Effective financial management is crucial for the sustainability and growth of any business, including a junk removal service. This chapter will guide you through the essentials of financial management from budgeting and cost control to revenue optimization and managing economic downturns. Mastering these aspects will ensure your business remains profitable and financially healthy over the long term.

9.1 Pricing Strategies

Setting the right prices for your services is fundamental to your business's profitability. Your pricing strategy should reflect the value you provide, cover your costs, and remain competitive within the market.

Key Considerations for Pricing

1. **Cost-Plus Pricing**: Calculate the total cost of providing your service, including direct costs like labor and fuel, and indirect costs like administration and marketing. Add a margin on top of these costs to ensure profitability.
2. **Market-Oriented Pricing**: Analyze your competitors' prices to ensure

your services are competitively priced. You may choose to position yourself as a premium service with higher prices if your service offers additional value, such as eco-friendly disposal practices or exceptional customer service.
3. **Dynamic Pricing**: Consider using dynamic pricing models where prices are adjusted based on demand, time of day, or specific customer requests. This can maximize earnings during peak times and increase job bookings during slower periods.
4. **Value-Based Pricing**: Price your services based on the perceived value to the customer rather than just the cost. This involves understanding the benefits your customers gain from your service, such as convenience, effectiveness, and customer experience.

Strategies to Enhance Pricing Flexibility

- **Transparent Pricing Communication**: Always be transparent with your pricing. Surprise charges can lead to customer dissatisfaction and damage your business's reputation.
- **Tiered Service Options**: Offer different levels of service at different price points to cater to a broader range of customers. For example, a basic service for budget-conscious customers and a premium service with additional features like same-day removal or cleanup services.

9.2 Cost Control

Managing your costs effectively is critical to maintaining your business's profitability. Cost control involves regularly reviewing and reducing expenses without compromising the quality of service.

Effective Cost Control Measures

1. **Regular Expense Reviews**: Conduct regular reviews of all business expenses to identify areas where you can cut costs or where spending is not yielding sufficient returns.
2. **Supplier Negotiations**: Regularly negotiate with suppliers and contractors to ensure you are getting the best prices for goods and services. Consider long-term contracts that might offer price stability or discounts.
3. **Invest in Efficiency**: Invest in technology and equipment that improve operational efficiency and reduce costs in the long term, such as fuel-efficient vehicles or route optimization software.
4. **Waste Reduction**: Implement practices to reduce waste in your operations, such as optimizing routes to reduce fuel consumption and training employees to minimize wasted time and resources.

9.3 Financial Forecasting

Financial forecasting involves predicting your future revenues, costs, and profits to make informed business decisions. Accurate forecasting can help you anticipate financial needs, identify potential financial challenges, and plan for future growth.

Techniques for Accurate Financial Forecasting

1. **Historical Analysis**: Use historical data to predict future performance, adjusting for any known changes in your business environment or operations.
2. **Scenario Planning**: Develop different scenarios (best, worst, and most likely cases) to understand potential outcomes and prepare for various eventualities.
3. **Regular Updates**: Update your forecasts regularly as new financial data becomes available and as market conditions change.

9.4 Handling Economic Downturns

Economic downturns can significantly impact your business. Being prepared can help you navigate through tough times without severe losses.

Strategies for Economic Resilience

1. **Financial Reserves**: Build a financial reserve to cushion your business during slow periods.
2. **Flexible Business Model**: Maintain flexibility in your business model so you can quickly adjust your operations and costs in response to economic downturns.
3. **Diversification**: Diversify your revenue streams to reduce reliance on a single source of income, which can provide stability when market conditions are unfavorable.

Key Takeaways:

- **Proactive Financial Management**: Stay on top of your financial management tasks, including pricing, cost control, and forecasting, to ensure long-term viability.
- **Build Economic Resilience**: Prepare for economic fluctuations by building resilience into your business model.
- **Continuous Improvement**: Regularly seek ways to improve financial management practices to enhance your business's profitability and sustainability.

Effective financial management is essential for the success of your junk removal business. By implementing robust pricing strategies, controlling costs, forecasting financial performance, and preparing for economic downturns, you can ensure that your business remains profitable and financially healthy. In the next chapter, we will explore future trends in the junk removal industry and how to prepare for upcoming changes and opportunities.

Chapter 10: Future Trends and Preparing for Change

Introduction to Chapter 10

As the junk removal industry continues to evolve, staying ahead of future trends is crucial for maintaining competitiveness and capitalizing on new opportunities. This chapter explores emerging trends in the industry and provides strategies for adapting and thriving in an ever-changing landscape.

10.1 Industry Innovations

Innovations in technology and business models are continuously reshaping the junk removal industry. Understanding these innovations can help you adapt and potentially lead the market.

Emerging Technological Trends

1. **Automation and Robotics**: The integration of automation and robotics in waste management is on the rise. Innovations such as automated sorting systems for recyclables and autonomous vehicles for pick-up and delivery services are beginning to penetrate the market, offering efficiencies that could transform operations.

2. **Advanced Recycling Technologies**: New recycling technologies that can handle more types of materials with greater efficiency are being developed. Staying abreast of these technologies and incorporating them into your operations can enhance your recycling capabilities and appeal to environmentally conscious consumers.
3. **Internet of Things (IoT)**: IoT technology is increasingly being used to monitor waste levels, optimize routes, and manage fleet operations more efficiently. Implementing IoT solutions can lead to significant cost savings and improved service quality.

Strategies for Leveraging Innovations

- **Continuous Learning**: Keep yourself and your team educated about new technologies and industry innovations through workshops, seminars, and online courses.
- **Invest in Pilot Projects**: Experiment with new technologies on a small scale through pilot projects to evaluate their impact and feasibility before full-scale implementation.
- **Collaborate with Tech Companies**: Partner with technology providers to tailor their solutions to your specific needs, ensuring that you benefit from the latest innovations.

10.2 Adapting to Consumer Behavior Changes

Consumer expectations and behaviors are constantly evolving, often driven by broader social and economic trends. Adapting to these changes is vital for maintaining relevance and customer loyalty.

Key Behavioral Trends

1. **Increased Environmental Awareness**: Consumers are becoming more environmentally conscious and expect companies to demonstrate a commitment to sustainable practices.
2. **Demand for Transparency**: There is a growing demand for transparency in pricing and operations. Consumers want to know exactly what they are paying for and how their waste is being handled.
3. **Preference for Customization**: Today's consumers expect services that are tailored to their specific needs. Offering customizable service options can enhance customer satisfaction and retention.

Strategies for Adapting to Consumer Trends

- **Enhance Sustainability Practices**: Continuously improve your sustainability initiatives and communicate these efforts clearly to your customers.
- **Implement Transparent Pricing Models**: Ensure that your pricing is clear and straightforward. Consider using pricing software that allows customers to get detailed quotes online based on their specific needs.
- **Offer Personalized Services**: Use customer data to offer personalized services. For example, you could provide subscription-based models where customers can choose how often they need junk removal services based on their output.

10.3 Regulatory Updates

Staying compliant with regulations is not only about adhering to the law but also about protecting your business and your customers. Regulations in the junk removal industry can change frequently, particularly those related to environmental impact and waste disposal.

Strategies for Staying Updated with Regulations

- **Regular Reviews**: Conduct regular reviews of relevant local, state, and federal regulations. Consider hiring a compliance officer or consulting with legal experts to stay informed.
- **Engage with Industry Associations**: Industry associations often provide resources and updates on regulatory changes. Being an active member can keep you informed and prepared for changes.
- **Advocate for Industry Interests**: Engage in advocacy efforts to influence policy-making that affects your industry. This can help ensure that new regulations are practical and beneficial for your business.

10.4 Long-Term Vision

Developing a long-term vision for your junk removal business involves anticipating future challenges and opportunities and planning strategically for growth and adaptation.

Strategies for Long-Term Planning

- **Scenario Planning**: Use scenario planning to anticipate potential future developments in the industry and economy. Prepare strategies for different scenarios to ensure flexibility and resilience.
- **Invest in Continuous Improvement**: Make continuous improvement a core aspect of your business philosophy. Regularly seek ways to enhance your services, reduce costs, and improve customer satisfaction.
- **Focus on Core Values**: Ensure that your long-term plans align with your company's core values. This alignment helps maintain consistency and authenticity, which are crucial for long-term success.

Key Takeaways:

- **Anticipate and Adapt**: Stay proactive about learning and adapting to

trends and changes in the industry.
- **Invest in Innovation**: Embrace innovation as a means to improve efficiency and appeal to modern consumers.
- **Plan Strategically**: Develop a flexible long-term strategy that allows your business to grow and evolve in a changing market.

Understanding and preparing for future trends is essential for the sustained success of your junk removal business. By staying informed, adaptable, and forward-thinking, you can navigate changes effectively and seize new opportunities as they arise.

Conclusion: Harnessing the Right Tools and Partnerships for Success

As we close this comprehensive guide on transforming your junk removal business from a mere startup to a thriving enterprise, it's crucial to recognize the importance of leveraging innovative tools and strategic partnerships. "From Clutter to Cash" has equipped you with the necessary knowledge and strategies to navigate the complexities of the junk removal industry. Now, let's ensure you have access to the best resources to implement these strategies effectively.

ClutterQuote: The quintessential tool for any junk removal entrepreneur, ClutterQuote simplifies the process of service estimation and booking, allowing you to respond quickly and accurately to customer inquiries. Its technology streamlines operations, reducing overhead and enhancing customer satisfaction. By integrating ClutterQuote into your business model, you can ensure a smoother, more efficient service that meets the modern consumer's expectations for speed and convenience. For more information on this, go to: https://www.clutterquote.com/

Roo & Wolf Ventures: For those looking to expand their business or explore new market opportunities, Roo & Wolf Ventures offers a strategic partnership that could prove invaluable. Specializing in business growth and strategic investment, they can provide the guidance and resources needed to scale your operations effectively and sustainably. Consider their expertise as a catalyst for taking your business to the next level. For more information on this, go to: https://www.rooandwolfventures.com/

EnFuegoMedia: In today's digital world, a robust online presence is indispensable. EnFuegoMedia can amplify your digital marketing efforts, ensuring that your business stands out in a crowded market. From optimizing your website for search engines to managing your social media presence, their tailored marketing strategies can attract more customers and build your brand online. For more information on this, go to: https://leadgenerationseoservices.com/

As you move forward, remember that the foundation of a successful junk removal business lies in your commitment to quality, efficiency, and adaptability. ClutterQuote, Roo & Wolf Ventures, and EnFuegoMedia represent just a few of the tools and partnerships that can facilitate these attributes. By choosing the right allies and embracing technology, your business is not only equipped to handle today's challenges but is also poised for future success.

Together, let's transform the clutter into opportunities, driving your junk removal business forward with innovation and strategic insight. Embrace these tools and partnerships, and watch as your business reaches new heights of success.

www.ingramcontent.com/pod-product-compliance
Lightning Source LLC
Chambersburg PA
CBHW070353230526
45471CB00006B/2541